AZERBAIJAN: HUMAN RIGHTS

EXECUTIVE SUMMARY

The Azerbaijani constitution provides for a republic with a presidential form of government. Legislative authority is vested in the Milli Mejlis (parliament). The president dominated the executive, legislative, and judicial branches of government. The October 9 presidential and 2010 parliamentary elections did not meet a number of key standards of the OSCE for democratic elections. Although there were more than 50 political parties, the president's party, the Yeni Azerbaijan Party, dominated the political system. Separatists, with Armenia's support, continued to control most of Nagorno-Karabakh and seven other Azerbaijani territories. The final status of Nagorno-Karabakh remained the subject of international mediation by the OSCE Minsk Group, cochaired by Russia, France, and the United States. Authorities maintained effective control over the security forces. Security forces committed human rights abuses.

The most significant human rights problems during the year were:

- Increased restrictions on freedoms of expression, assembly, and association, including intimidation, arrest, and use of force against journalists and human rights and democracy activists online and offline. Prior to the official presidential election campaign period, the government approved only a handful of applications for peaceful protests, limited approved demonstrations mainly to inconvenient locations, forcefully dispersed unsanctioned protests, and often detained demonstrators. Five opposition rallies, however, took place in Baku at an accessible site during and after the campaign period with limited or no interference. Amendments adopted during the year further restricted NGO financing. Following the October 9 presidential election, authorities launched a criminal investigation against two election monitoring NGOs, the Election Monitoring and Democracy Studies Center (EMDS) and the International Cooperation of Volunteers (ICV) Public Union, arrested the EMDS chairman, and banned the EMDS executive director and the ICV chairman from leaving the country.

- Restrictions on the right of citizens to change their government peacefully. Flaws in the conduct of the October 9 presidential election included a repressive political environment leading up to election day, lack of a level playing field among candidates, significant shortcomings throughout all stages of election-day processes, and a complaints and appeals process lacking impartiality.

- Unfair administration of justice, including increased reports of arbitrary arrest and detention, politically motivated imprisonment, lack of due process, executive influence over the judiciary, and lengthy pretrial detention for individuals perceived as a threat by government officials, while crimes against such individuals or their family members went unpunished. Authorities failed to provide due legal process with regard to property rights, resulting in forced evictions, demolition of buildings on dubious eminent domain grounds, and inadequate compensation for property taken by the state. Allegations of widespread corruption at all levels continued, although the presidential administration took significant steps to decrease corruption by public service providers in Baku.

Other human rights problems reported during the year included abuse in the military that resulted in 69 noncombat deaths, harsh and sometimes life-threatening prison conditions, continued arbitrary invasions of privacy, restrictions on the religious freedom of some unregistered Muslim and Christian groups, constraints on political participation, continued official impediments to the registration of human rights NGOs, violence against women, and trafficking in persons.

The government failed to take steps to prosecute or punish most officials who committed human rights abuses. Impunity remained a problem.

Section 1. Respect for the Integrity of the Person, Including Freedom from:

a. Arbitrary or Unlawful Deprivation of Life

There were no reports that the government or its agents committed arbitrary or unlawful killings.

Abuse in the military was widespread and at times resulted in death. Local human rights organizations reported at least 81 deaths in the military, of which 69 were not related to combat, including soldiers killed by fellow servicemen and suicides. Impunity for abuses continued.

In one example that resulted in protests against noncombat deaths in the military, the Ministry of Defense claimed that an 18-year-old conscript, Ceyhun Qubadov, died of heart failure on January 7, although Qubadov's mother asserted he had been beaten to death and released photos of his wounded body on the internet. The Military Prosecutor's Office opened a criminal case on charges of negligence, arrested two low-ranking officers, dismissed two officers, and downgraded one officer.

Separatists, with Armenia's support, continued to control most of Nagorno-Karabakh and seven other Azerbaijani territories. During the year shooting incidents continued along the militarized line of contact separating the two sides in the Nagorno-Karabakh conflict and resulted in numerous casualties on both sides. Figures for civilian casualties along the line of contact were not available.

b. Disappearance

There were no reports of politically motivated disappearances during the year.

The State Committee on the Captive and Missing reported that 4,037 citizens were registered during the year as missing persons as the result of the Nagorno-Karabakh conflict. The International Committee of the Red Cross (ICRC) facilitated the return of two civilians to Armenia in March.

The ICRC continued to process cases of persons missing in connection with the Nagorno-Karabakh conflict and worked with the government to develop a consolidated list of missing persons. As of November 8, according to tracing requests made by relatives to the ICRC, 4,620 persons remained unaccounted for as a result of the conflict, with the ICRC handling 4,220 cases in Azerbaijan, including Nagorno-Karabakh.

The ICRC continued to assist prisoners of war and civilian internees (POWs/CIs) and conducted monthly visits throughout the year to ensure their protection under international humanitarian law. The ICRC regularly facilitated the exchange of Red Cross messages between POWs/CIs and their families to help them re-establish and maintain contact.

c. Torture and Other Cruel, Inhuman, or Degrading Treatment or Punishment

While the constitution and criminal code prohibit such practices and provide for penalties of up to 10 years' imprisonment, domestic human rights monitors reported that security forces abused 111 persons in custody during the year (including a number of reported instances of torture), compared with 141 in 2012. Reports indicated that most mistreatment took place while detainees were in police stations and that abuse ceased once detainees moved to pretrial detention facilities. In one notable exception, human rights activists reported that, on September 11, authorities beat Ilkin Rustamzade, a detainee in the Kurdakhani detention facility, for publishing an article in an opposition newspaper. As of year's end, there was no investigation of the allegation.

Impunity remained a problem. Authorities reportedly maintained a de facto ban on independent forensic examinations of detainees who claimed mistreatment and delayed their access to an attorney.

Reports continued that authorities used torture or other mistreatment to coerce confessions. For example, there were allegations that authorities forced N!DA (which means exclamation point in Azeri) youth movement members Shahin Novruzlu, Bakhtiyar Guliyev, and Mammad Azizov to appear on March 9 on state television reading prepared "confessions" that they had planned to use violence to foment revolution at a March 10 protest against deaths in the army. According to Human Rights Watch (HRW), Azizov informed his lawyer that Ministry of National Security officers beat him after he retracted his "confession." Azizov reportedly could not walk for four days and lost hearing in one ear.

Efforts to coerce confessions reportedly at times included threats of rape.

Local observers reported widespread bullying and abuse in military units during the year, including physical and sexual abuse. In one example five soldiers and an officer beat and shot soldier Jamil Huseynzade on October 28 and left him in a canal in Tovuz District. A passerby found the soldier and took him to the hospital. The Military Prosecutor's Office opened a criminal investigation.

Prison and Detention Center Conditions

Many prisoners experienced harsh detention conditions, some of which were life threatening. While the government continued to construct new facilities, some Soviet-era facilities did not meet international standards. Overcrowding, inadequate nutrition, deficient heating and ventilation, and poor medical care combined to make the spread of infectious diseases a problem in some facilities.

Physical Conditions: The prison population numbered approximately 20,000 persons, approximately the same as in 2012. Of these 13.5 percent were in pretrial detention; 2.3 percent were women. Authorities held men and women together in pretrial detention facilities in separate blocks but housed women in separate prison facilities after they were sentenced. Local NGO observers reported that female prisoners lived in better conditions than male prisoners, were monitored more frequently, and had greater access to training and other activities. Although minors were also supposed to be held in separate facilities, international monitors observed some children being held with adults in 2012. Prisoners may be held in juvenile institutions until the age of 20.

Authorities reported increased efforts to ensure adequate physical exercise for prisoners and opportunities to work or receive training. Authorities at times limited visits by attorneys and family members. Former prisoners reported guards punished prisoners with beatings or by holding them in isolation cells. Local and international monitors continued to report poor conditions at the maximum security Qobustan Prison.

The Ministry of Justice reported that 111 persons died in detention in 2012. The ministry reported that 84 of the deaths were in medical facilities and due to medical conditions. Tuberculosis remained the leading cause of death in prison facilities in 2012, followed by cancer and heart disease. The Ministry of Internal Affairs reported two deaths in pretrial detention facilities during 2013. Both were reportedly suicides. The ministry took action against 11 employees for the incidents.

The majority of prisons and detention centers provided access to potable water.

Administration: Prison recordkeeping appeared adequate. Prisoners had access to family visitors, although in some cases authorities limited this access. Authorities permitted religious observance. While most prisoners reported that they could submit complaints to judicial authorities and the Ombudsman's Office without censorship, domestic NGOs reported that some prisoners in high-security facilities experienced difficulty submitting such complaints. Prison authorities regularly read prisoners' correspondence. The national human rights ombudsman received a variety of human rights complaints, including from prisoners. While the Ombudsman's Office reported systematic visits and investigations into complaints, NGOs reported a lack of interest in fully addressing prisoner complaints.

Independent Monitoring: The government permitted some prison visits by international and local humanitarian and human rights groups, including the ICRC, the Council of Europe's Committee for the Prevention of Torture, the OSCE, the EU (accompanied by representatives of some of its members' embassies), and the Azerbaijan Committee against Torture. The Ministry of Justice required the Azerbaijan Committee against Torture to obtain prior notification before visiting its facilities, but the Ministry of Internal Affairs continued to allow the committee immediate access to its pretrial detention centers. Authorities generally permitted the ICRC access to the POWs/CIs who were held in connection with the conflict over Nagorno-Karabakh as well as to detainees held in facilities under the authority of the Ministries of Justice, Internal Affairs, and National Security.

A joint government-human rights community prison monitoring group, known as the Public Committee, was able to gain access to prisons without prior notification to the penitentiary service. On some occasions during the year, however, other groups reportedly experienced difficulty obtaining access, even with prior notification.

Improvements: According to the ICRC, the government undertook significant efforts to improve detention conditions by building new facilities and modernizing existing detention centers. The Ministry of Internal Affairs reported that it opened five new detention facilities and renovated eight facilities during the year.

d. Arbitrary Arrest or Detention

Although the law prohibits arbitrary arrest and detention, the government generally did not observe these prohibitions, and impunity remained a problem.

Role of the Police and Security Apparatus

The Ministry of Internal Affairs and the Ministry of National Security are responsible for internal security and report directly to the president. The Ministry of Internal Affairs oversees local police forces and maintains internal civil defense troops. The Ministry of National Security oversees intelligence and counterintelligence activities and has a separate internal security force. NGOs reported detentions by both ministries of individuals who exercised their rights to fundamental freedoms, including freedom of expression.

Police crowd control tactics varied during the year. Police used excessive force in some cases during protests that took place at the beginning of the year, during which police and internal security troops reportedly used rubber bullets, tear gas, and water cannons. In certain cases police detained peaceful protestors and used excessive force against them.

While security forces generally acted with impunity, the Ministry of Internal Affairs stated that it took action against 241 employees during the year for groundlessly detaining individuals. The ministry further reported that it brought 172 cases of misconduct against ministry officials accused of violating citizens' rights.

Arrest Procedures and Treatment of Detainees

The law states that persons detained, arrested, or accused of a crime should be advised immediately of their rights, given the reason for their arrest, and accorded due process. The government did not always respect these provisions.

While the law allows police to detain and question an individual for 48 hours without a warrant, police detained individuals for several days without warrants. Legal experts asserted that in other instances judges issued warrants after the fact. There were no reports of detainees not being promptly informed of the charges against them, although in several cases, authorities drastically amended charges later. Such cases included 10 individuals considered to be prisoners of conscience by Amnesty International (AI). Of the 10, two were democratic opposition leaders, seven were N!DA democracy youth activists, and one was a Free Youth democracy youth activist (see sections 1.c. and 1.e.). Following amended charges all 10 faced up to 12 years' imprisonment at year's end.

The law provides for access to a lawyer from the time of detention. Access to lawyers was poor, particularly outside of Baku. Although entitled to legal counsel by law, indigent detainees often did not have such access. Family members reported that authorities occasionally restricted family-member visits, especially to persons in pretrial detention, and occasionally withheld information about detainees. Days sometimes passed before families could obtain any information about detained relatives.

Politically sensitive and other suspects were at times held incommunicado by police for several hours or sometimes days; there were reports of an emerging trend in which authorities frequently denied lawyers access to clients in both politically motivated and routine cases. In one case police reportedly held religious scholar and activist Taleh Bagirzade incommunicado for a week after his arrest on March 31. A week before his arrest, Bagirzade reportedly delivered a sermon at a mosque criticizing the government. On November 1, after a hasty trial, authorities sentenced Bagirzade to two years in prison on charges of drug possession.

There was no formal, functioning bail system, although authorities sometimes permitted individuals to vouch for detainees, enabling their conditional release during pretrial investigation.

Arbitrary Arrest: Arbitrary arrest, often based on spurious charges of resisting police, illegal possession of drugs or weapons, or inciting public disorder, remained a problem throughout the year. Local NGOs, AI, and HRW criticized the government for arresting individuals exercising their fundamental rights and noted that the authorities frequently fabricated charges against them. In particular, police detained members of democratic opposition movements or political parties that attempted to hold peaceful political demonstrations. For example, authorities arrested youth and other democracy activists who called for, organized, or participated in peaceful demonstrations during the first half of the year. These activists included seven members of the N!DA youth movement (Bakhtiyar Guliyev, Mammad Azizov, Rashad Hasanov, Rashadat Akhundov, Shahin Novruzlu, Uzeyir Mammadli, and Zaur Gurbanli), one Free Youth activist (Ilkin Rustamzade), and two activists in youth branches of political parties (Dashgin Malikov and Rasul Mursalov) (see sections 1.c. and 1.e.). Additionally, on November 26, police arrested Facebook activist Abdul Abilov and subsequently charged him with illegal possession of drugs. Independent media speculated that Abilov's criticism of authorities led to his arrest. Observers also reported police violations of arrest and detention procedures.

Lengthy pretrial detention of up to 18 months occurred. The prosecutor general routinely extended the initial three-month pretrial detention period permitted by law in successive increments of several months until the government completed an investigation.

Amnesty: On May 7, the Milli Mejlis amnestied 2,000 prisoners. Of those released, NGOs considered only Ilgar Rzayev, who was arrested for protesting property rights violations which occurred prior to the 2012 Eurovision Song Contest, to have been a political prisoner.

On October 14, the president pardoned 153 prisoners. Human rights monitors viewed two of those released as political prisoners (see section 1.e.).

e. Denial of Fair Public Trial

Although the law provides for an independent judiciary, judges did not function independently of the executive branch. The judiciary remained corrupt and inefficient. Verdicts were largely unrelated to the evidence presented during the trial.

The executive branch continued to exert a strong influence over the judiciary. The Ministry of Justice controlled the Judicial Legal Council (JLC). The JLC appoints a judicial selection committee (six judges, a prosecutor, an advocate, a JLC representative, a Ministry of Justice representative, and a legal scholar) which administers the judicial selection examination and oversees the year-long judicial training and selection process.

Credible reports indicated that judges and prosecutors took instruction from the presidential administration and the Ministry of Justice, particularly in cases of interest to international observers. There continued to be credible allegations that judges routinely accepted bribes. The ministry reported that as of November 1, the JLC suspended two judges and disciplined nine others.

Trial Procedures

The law provides for public trials except in cases involving state, commercial, or professional secrets or confidential, personal, or family matters. While the law provides for the presumption of innocence in criminal cases; the right of the defendant to review evidence, confront witnesses, and present evidence at the trial; the right of indigent defendants to a court-approved attorney; and the right of both defendants and prosecutors to appeal, authorities did not always respect these provisions. Defendants had the right to be informed promptly of charges against them in detail, with free interpretation if necessary.

Judges often failed to read verdicts publicly or give the reasoning behind their decisions, leaving the accused without knowledge of the reasoning behind the judgment.

Jury trials were not used. Foreign and domestic observers usually were allowed to attend trials, except those involving espionage or treason charges. The use of small courtrooms with inadequate seating and last-minute changes in starting times prevented public attendance at some hearings. Information regarding trial times and locations was generally available, although there were some exceptions, particularly in the Court of Grave Crimes.

Although the constitution prescribes equal status for prosecutors and defense attorneys, prosecutors' privileges and rights outweighed those of the defense. Judges reserved the right to remove defense lawyers in civil cases for "good cause." In criminal proceedings judges may remove defense lawyers because of a conflict of interest or if a defendant requests a change of counsel. Judges often favored prosecutors when assessing motions, oral statements, and evidence submitted by defense counsel. For example, in the case of *Tolishi-Sado* newspaper editor in chief Hilal Mammadov, authorities on numerous occasions prevented lawyers from meeting with their client. Additionally, judges often rejected the defense attorneys' motions and favored prosecutors. Human rights and media freedom NGOs and the international community considered Mammadov, who was sentenced on September 27 to five years in prison on charges of treason, incitement of ethnic hatred, and drug possession, to be a political prisoner.

The law limits representation in criminal cases to members of the country's government-influenced Collegium (bar association). As of November 1, the number of lawyers who were Collegium members increased to 834 defense lawyers from 818 in 2012. Nonetheless, the number of defense lawyers willing to accept sensitive cases reportedly declined during the year due to pressure from authorities, including from the Collegium's presidium. Examples of such pressure included the sentencing of lawyer Bakhtiyar Mammadov to eight years in prison on February 27. AI considered Bakhtiyar a prisoner of conscience, and the Human Rights Club considered him a political prisoner. There were also reports of police violence against lawyers. The proportion of Collegium lawyers practicing outside the capital remained relatively steady at approximately 25 percent.

The presidium is the managing body of the Collegium and has the authority to suspend or expel lawyers in conjunction with its disciplinary committee. During the year the presidium suspended one lawyer. On May 8, the presidium disbarred lawyer Aslan Ismayilov and terminated his legal activities. Ismayilov led several high-profile anticorruption and other sensitive cases and faced threats and intimidation from authorities. HRW reported that on May 30, a Ministry of Internal Affairs' Organized Crime Unit official slapped Ismayilov and warned that he faced imprisonment if he did not "behave." The investigator then warned that "if you value your life, you'll be quiet." Throughout the second half of May, Ismayilov had publicly alleged that police beat blogger Rashad Ramazanov while he was in the Organized Crime Unit's custody. On September 10, the Narimanov District Court disbarred Ismayilov.

The constitution prohibits the use of illegally obtained evidence. Despite some defendants' claims that authorities obtained testimony through torture or abuse, courts did not dismiss cases based on claims of abuse, and there was no independent forensic investigator to determine the occurrence of abuse. Judges often ignored claims of police mistreatment. Investigations often focused on obtaining confessions rather than gathering physical evidence against suspects. Serious crimes brought before the courts most often ended in conviction, since judges generally required only a minimal level of proof and collaborated closely with prosecutors. When a judge determined that the evidence presented was not sufficient to convict a defendant, a case could be returned to the prosecutor for additional investigation, effectively giving the prosecutor another chance to obtain a conviction.

With the exception of the Court of Grave Crimes, courts often failed to provide interpreters. Courts are entitled to contract interpreters during hearings, with the expenses covered by the state budget.

There were no verbatim transcripts of judicial proceedings; court testimony, oral arguments, and judicial decisions were not recorded. Instead the court officer generally took notes that tended to be sparse and decided their content.

The country has a military court system with civilian judges. The military court retains original jurisdiction over any case related to war or military service.

Political Prisoners and Detainees

During the year local and international NGOs maintained that the government continued to hold political prisoners and detainees; estimates of the number varied from dozens to 143. NGOs' lists of political prisoners and detainees included journalists (see section 2.a.), human rights defenders (see sections 1.e. and 3), secular and religious opposition figures (see sections 1.d., 2.b., and 3), and youth activists (see sections 1.c. and 1.d.).

In one case on February 4, authorities arrested Ilgar Mammadov, the chairman of the REAL Movement and presidential candidate aspirant, and Musavat Party journalist and Deputy Chairman Tofig Yagublu and charged them with organizing social disorder and resisting authorities. Mammadov and Yagublu had gone to the city of Ismayilli in late January to gather information after antigovernment riots began there. The international community and 167 public figures in the country recognized them – along with Anar Mammadli (see section 3) and others – as prisoners of conscience and called for their immediate release. Their trial began November 4 and continued at year's end.

On October 14, President Aliyev pardoned former minister of economic development Farhad Aliyev and his brother, AzPetrol President Rafiq Aliyev, who were widely viewed as political prisoners. Authorities arrested both in 2005 on allegations of coup plotting but ultimately convicted them of embezzlement. In the days leading to the October 9 presidential election, Farhad Aliyev publicly endorsed President Aliyev's re-election.

By law political prisoners are entitled to the same rights as other prisoners. Nevertheless, restrictions vary on a prison-to-prison basis. International humanitarian organizations received access to political prisoners.

Civil Judicial Procedures and Remedies

Citizens have the right to bring lawsuits seeking damages for, or cessation of, human rights violations. The law does not provide for a jury trial in civil matters; the judge decides all trials. District courts have jurisdiction over civil matters in their first hearing; the Court of Appeals and then the Supreme Court addresses appeals.   As with criminal trials, all citizens have the right to appeal to the European Court of Human Rights (ECHR) within six months after exhausting all domestic legal options, consisting of an appeal to and ruling by the Supreme Court.

Regional Human Rights Court Decisions

Citizens continued to exercise the right to appeal to the ECHR and brought claims of government violations of commitments under the European Convention on Human Rights.   The government's compliance with ECHR decisions was mixed.

f. Arbitrary Interference with Privacy, Family, Home, or Correspondence

The law prohibits arbitrary invasions of privacy and monitoring of correspondence and other private communications.   The government did not respect these legal prohibitions.

While the constitution allows for searches of residences only with a court order or in cases specifically provided for by law, authorities often conducted searches without warrants.   It was widely believed that the Ministry of National Security and the Ministry of Internal Affairs monitored telephone and internet communications, particularly those of foreigners, youth figures active online, some political and business figures, and persons engaged in international communication.

Police continued to intimidate, harass, and sometimes arrest family members of suspected criminals and political opposition members as well as employees and leaders of certain NGOs and their family members.   For example, the Human Rights Club considered Elnur Seyidov a political detainee.   Detained since March 2012, Seyidov was opposition Popular Front Party chairman Ali Kerimli's brother-in-law.   On October 29, the Court of Grave Crimes sentenced Seyidov to seven-and-a-half years in prison.   In another case widely considered politically motivated, authorities incarcerated Kerimli's son, Turkel, for 25 days in the weeks preceding the October presidential election.   He was one of three sons of prominent opposition party or movement leaders detained or physically assaulted with impunity during the year.

Citizens reported that authorities fired individuals from their jobs in retaliation for the political or civic activities of family members.   For example, NGOs reported that the wife and son of writer Akram Aylisli were fired from their public sector jobs in early February.   Their forced "voluntary" resignations occurred during a smear campaign against Aylisli for the condemnation of Azerbaijani violence against

Armenians in his novel *Stone Dreams*.

NGOs reported that authorities did not respect the laws governing eminent domain and expropriation of property. Homeowners often received compensation well below market value and had little legal recourse. Domestic monitors reported that the number of property rights complaints they received continued to rise compared with previous years. NGOs reported that many citizens did not trust the country's court system and were therefore reluctant to pursue compensation claims.

Disabled Nagorno-Karabakh war veteran Zaur Hasanov set himself on fire on December 25 to protest a court order upholding the unlawful seizure of his land and demolition of his family's café by the head of the Azerbaijan Trade Unions Confederation, member of parliament (MP) Sattar Mehbaliyev. Hasanov died from his injuries on December 28.

According to a local NGO, the multi-year construction of the Oghuz-Gabala-Baku water pipeline reportedly displaced 16,000 individuals across eight regions, with little compensation. Despite a court verdict providing for compensation of landowners, by the end of 2012, the national water management agency Azersu had provided monetary compensation to only two landowners. As of year's end, litigation on property rights violations continued in various courts.

Section 2. Respect for Civil Liberties, Including:

a. Freedom of Speech and Press

While the law provides for freedom of speech and press and specifically prohibits press censorship, the government often did not respect these rights. The government continued to limit freedom of speech and media independence. Journalists faced intimidation and were beaten and imprisoned. NGOs considered at least 12 journalists and bloggers to be political prisoners or detainees. In a joint press release issued October 8, 22 domestic and international NGOs described the environment for the media and those who expressed political opposition as "increasingly restrictive."

Freedom of Speech: The constitution provides for freedom of speech, but government restrictions of this right increased regarding subjects it considered politically sensitive. Citing in part an increased number of arrests of government critics on what it termed "bogus charges," HRW reported on September 2 that the government had intensified its efforts to crack down on peaceful dissent since mid-2012. During the year authorities prevented youth and opposition activists from holding peaceful demonstrations in Baku and detained those they suspected of participating in such activities. The incarceration of persons who attempted to exercise freedom of speech raised concerns about authorities' use of the judicial system to punish dissent. Authorities also attempted to impede discussion in April by closing the facility of the Free Thought University, a nonpartisan forum established by young activists to facilitate the development of analytical skills and independent thinking. Additionally, the government attempted to impede criticism by monitoring political and civil society meetings.

Press Freedoms: A number of opposition and independent print and online media outlets operated during the year, expressing a wide variety of views on government policies. Newspaper circulation rates remained low, not surpassing 5,000 in most cases. Credible reports indicated that opposition newspapers were available outside of Baku only in limited numbers due to the refusal of a number of distributors to carry them. On October 17, the Baku metro banned the sale of three opposition newspapers: *Azadlig, Yeni Musavat, and Gundem Kheber.* On November 15, authorities amended the order to include sales of all printed materials in metro stations. *Azadliq* – long under pressure – ceased publication briefly in November but restarted after receiving public financial support. Authorities froze *Azadliq*'s bank accounts in November due to the newspaper's failure to pay large defamation fines imposed by courts in response to lawsuits filed by government allies. In late December the newspaper reported it could again access its accounts.

The broadcast media adhered to a progovernment line in their news coverage prior to the October 9 presidential election. According to the OSCE's Office for Democratic Institutions and Human Rights (ODIHR), President Aliyev, the incumbent, received 92 percent of presidential candidate coverage on six television stations that its experts monitored in the pre-election period.

Foreign broadcasters, including the Voice of America, Radio Free Europe/Radio Liberty, and the BBC, remained prohibited from broadcasting on FM radio frequencies.

A local NGO monitoring media freedom stated that 12 journalists and bloggers were in prison or facing criminal charges at year's end. For example, on September 17, authorities detained journalist and activist Parviz Hashimli and subsequently sentenced him to two months' pretrial detention on charges of smuggling large arms and ammunition from Iran to Azerbaijan. Authorities reportedly denied him access to a lawyer for several days. Human rights and media freedom NGOs considered him a political detainee. On November 25, Hashimli initiated a hunger strike to protest substandard detention conditions and authorities' refusal to let him see his family. In mid-December Hashimli stated that authorities had tortured him, and his attorney and family stated that authorities frequently subjected him to psychological pressure and physical mistreatment. The court dismissed Hashimli's claims of torture, calling them "unsubstantiated."

On March 12, the Court of Grave Crimes sentenced *Khural* editor Avaz Zeynalli, whose reporting exposed corruption within the government, to nine years' imprisonment on bribery-related charges. Human rights and media freedom NGOs considered him a political prisoner.

On November 13, a district court sentenced *Nota Bene* editor Sardar Alibeyli to four years in prison for hooliganism. Civil society activists believed police arrested Alibeyli for his criticism of the government. AI considered Aliybeyli a prisoner of conscience.

Violence and Harassment: A media-monitoring NGO reported 61 incidents involving verbal or physical assaults on journalists during the year, compared with 71 such incidents in 2012. On February 15, for example, the editor in chief of *Unikal* newspaper, Asef Rzayev, reported intimidation from a hotel owner after the newspaper published articles critical of his establishment in Absheron District. Some journalists also reported receiving death threats. For example, *Radio Liberty* journalist Yafez Hasanov reported receiving death threats throughout the year. Despite his complaints authorities took no practical steps to stop the perpetrators.

The government used the media to harass and discredit those with dissenting views. In one prominent example, a progovernment website in April posted a sexually explicit video of a woman it claimed was investigative journalist Khadija Ismailova. Ismailova asserted that the video was fabricated and part of a smear campaign begun against her by state-controlled or progovernment press outlets in 2012. On July 26, a second website posted intimate videos of Ismailova, apparently covertly filmed in her apartment. Throughout the year newspapers officially affiliated with the ruling party appeared to conduct an orchestrated smear campaign against her, publishing links to websites posting the videos and articles attacking her and her family. Ismailova's work linked the president's family to corruption. The case provoked strong international and local condemnation, with many observers citing it as a continuing attempt to intimidate a journalist.

There were reports that police harassed, and in some cases physically harmed, journalists trying to cover numerous protests during the year. There were no indications that authorities held any police officers accountable for physical assaults on journalists in recent years.

Journalists and media rights leaders continued to call for an investigation into the 2011 killing of journalist Rafiq Tagi, against whom an Iranian cleric, Grand Ayatollah Fazel Lankarani, had issued a fatwa, and the 2005 killing of independent editor and journalist Elmar Huseynov.

Lawsuits suspected of being politically motivated were also used to intimidate journalists and media outlets. The majority of independent and opposition newspapers remained in a precarious financial situation and continued to have problems paying wages, taxes, and periodic court fines. Most relied on political parties, influential sponsors, or the State Media Fund for financing.

The government prohibited some state libraries from subscribing to opposition newspapers, prohibited state businesses from buying advertising in opposition newspapers, and pressured private businesses not to advertise in them. As a result paid advertising was largely absent in opposition media. Political commentators noted that these practices reduced the wages that opposition and independent outlets could pay to their journalists, allowing progovernment outlets to hire away quality staff. Additionally, international media monitoring reports indicated intimidation by officials of the Ministry of Taxes that further limited the independence of the media.

Local observers reported the demolition of newspaper kiosks by local authorities resulted in a large decrease in the distribution of opposition newspapers. Observers reported that the kiosks built to replace them distributed a small number of progovernment newspapers and served more as convenience stores than newsstands.

Censorship or Content Restriction: Most media practiced self-censorship and avoided topics considered politically sensitive.

Beginning in April RFE/RL's Azerbaijani-language satellite programming was subjected to targeted signal interference, which it concluded was deliberate. Two opposition-oriented satellite broadcasts from other providers also encountered difficulties transmitting into the country. On July 9, American-British human rights activist Rebecca Vincent reported that all three broadcasters appeared to have been targeted for transmitting alternative news coverage into the country.

The National Television and Radio Council requires that local, privately owned television and radio stations not rebroadcast entire news programs of foreign origin.

Libel Laws/National Security: Libel remains a criminal offense. The law allows for large fines and up to three years' imprisonment for persons convicted of libel. Defamation is also prohibited and is punishable by fines ranging from 100 to 1,000 manat ($125 to $1,250) and imprisonment for six months to three years. According to a local media rights organization, claims totaling approximately 4.7 million manat ($5.9 million) were brought against newspapers or their owners, with judgments totaling 145,000 manat ($181,000) awarded during the year.

Internet Freedom

The government generally did not restrict access to the internet, but it required internet service providers to be licensed and have formal agreements with the Ministry of Communications and Information Technologies. According to International Telecommunication Union statistics, approximately 70 percent of the country's population used the internet during the year.

On June 5, President Aliyev signed into law several amendments to the criminal code extending criminal penalties for libel and insult to the internet. The OSCE representative on freedom of the media, Dunja Mijatovic, and the Council of Europe commissioner for human rights, Nils Muiznieks, had called on the president not to sign these amendments. On July 30, the Astara District Court issued the first verdict implementing the June 5 amendments, sentencing Mikayil Talibov to one year of corrective (public) labor and payment of 20 percent of his income; the court also ordered him to post a Facebook statement recanting his online criticism of Access Bank. On November 25, however, an appeals court overturned Talibov's conviction and ordered the Astara District Court to reconsider the case.

There were strong indications that the government monitored internet communications of democracy activists. For example, at least 11 youth democracy activists detained or briefly jailed during the year frequently posted criticism of alleged government corruption and human rights abuses online. On November 13, the Court of Grave Crimes sentenced blogger Rashad Ramazanov to nine years in prison for drug possession. Civil society activists believed Ramazanov's criticism of the president and other authorities on Facebook prompted his arrest. AI considered Ramazanov a prisoner of conscience. In an October 8 joint press release signed by 22 human rights and press freedom NGOs, Maria Dahle of the Human Rights House Foundation stated, "Azerbaijani authorities target and punish individuals for the information they put on social media… and use the courts politically to sentence people to long-term imprisonment." In its annual report, *Freedom on the Net*, Freedom House acknowledged the country's vibrant and rapidly growing online community, while "those who speak out on the internet are more likely to face intimidation, threats, arrests, and fines from the state."

There were occasional reports of denial of service attacks on opposition and some independent advocacy NGO websites. For example, the websites of the opposition newspaper *Azadliq*, news portal site *Contact.az*, and RFE/RL suffered denial of service attacks, as did that of the Institute for Reporters' Freedom and Safety. In the exclave of Nakhchivan, website blockages were reportedly more common.

Academic Freedom and Cultural Events

The government on occasion restricted academic freedom.

Some domestic observers continued to raise concerns that the government's selection of participants for state-sponsored study abroad programs was biased and took political affiliation into account. The government denied the allegation and claimed its selection process was transparent.

Baku State University reportedly coerced history professor Altay Goyushov to resign in November due to Facebook posts critical of the government. Nevertheless, Goyushov returned to work after students protested against his resignation. Opposition party members continued to report difficulties in finding jobs teaching at schools and universities. In December Baku State University effectively deprived unified opposition presidential candidate Jamil Hasanli of his teaching position by refusing to assign classes to him. Additionally, Gafgaz University professor and former MP Gultakin Hajibayli reported pressure against her and her family members after she joined the opposition National Council of Democratic Forces (NCDF). Hajibayli ultimately resigned. Authorities fired most known opposition party members teaching in state educational institutions in previous years.

NGOs reported that local executive authorities occasionally prevented the expression of minority cultures, for example, by prohibiting cultural events.

b. Freedom of Peaceful Assembly and Association

Freedom of Assembly

While the law provides for freedom of assembly, the government severely restricted the right. With the exception of the immediate pre-election period and the weeks following the election, authorities severely restricted peaceful protests during the year, at times using force and detaining protesters. For example, during a peaceful January 12 protest in Baku, police reportedly detained approximately 100 persons.

On January 26, police used water cannons and tear gas to disperse a peaceful protest in Baku against officials' impunity in the town of Ismayilli. Police detained five persons, who local courts sentenced to between 13 and 15 days' detention. Twenty protestors were fined between 400 and 2,000 manat ($500 and $2,500).

On March 10, police in Baku used water cannons, rubber bullets, and tear gas to disperse a peaceful protest against the deaths of army conscripts. Police detained 100 persons and released them outside the city. Authorities sentenced four persons to six to seven days in administrative detention and fined 17 persons 400 to 600 manat ($500 to $750).

While the constitution stipulates that groups may peacefully assemble after notifying the relevant government body in advance, the government continued to interpret this provision as a requirement for prior permission. Local authorities continued to require all rallies to be preapproved and held at designated locations, mainly in inconvenient sites, although a popular Baku site was easily accessible by metro and bus. Most political parties and NGOs found such requirements unacceptable and believed them to be unconstitutional. Although the government permitted the opposition NCDF and other groups to hold public rallies in the weeks leading to and following the October 9 presidential election, authorities throughout the country routinely refused to acknowledge notifications, thereby effectively denying the freedom to assemble.

On May 2, the Milli Mejlis amended the law to raise the maximum length of administrative detention for misdemeanors generally from 15 days to three months, increase the maximum length of administrative detention for resisting police from 15 days to one month, and increase punishment for those who fail to follow a court order (including failure to pay a fine). The latter increased fines from 20 to 35 manat ($25 to $44) to 500 to 1,000 manat ($400 to $1,250) and also introduced a punishment of up to one month of administrative detention.

Authorities applied restrictions on unsanctioned protests arbitrarily, permitting protests against the political opposition even when advance notice had not been officially provided.

Freedom of Association

The constitution provides for freedom of association, although the law places some restrictions on this right, and amendments enacted during the year placed additional restrictions on NGO financing.

A number of legal provisions allow the government to regulate the activities of political parties, religious groups, businesses, and NGOs, including requiring NGOs to register with the Justice Ministry if they want to obtain "legal personality" status. Although the law requires the government to act on registration applications within 30 days (or within an additional 30 days, if further investigation is required) of receipt, vague, cumbersome, and nontransparent registration procedures continued to result in long delays that limited citizens' right to associate. Other laws restrict freedom of association, for example, by requiring deputy heads of NGO branches to be Azerbaijani citizens if the head of the branch is a foreigner and requiring foreign NGOs to sign an agreement with the government before opening a branch.

On March 12, parliament adopted amendments to several laws affecting grants and donations, creating a de facto prohibition on NGOs receiving cash donations and making it nearly impossible for NGOs to receive anonymous donations or to solicit contributions from the general public. The amended laws increased penalties for NGOs that fail to register a grant and introduced penalties for implementation of projects with a grant contract, for failure to include donation information in financial reports, for donors giving cash donations to NGOs exceeding 200 manat ($250), and for NGOs that receive cash donations.

Parliament passed amendments December 17 to the laws on NGOs, grants, registration of legal entities, and code of administrative offenses, that impose new restrictions on NGO activities. The package of amendments closes loopholes for the operations of unregistered, independent, and foreign NGOs. Changes include new registration-related obligations, increased grant-related and other reporting requirements, and expanded punishments for perceived noncompliance with local laws, government investigations, and information requests. The amendments awaited the president's signature at year's end. Members of over 30 respected NGOs and some in the international community urged the president not to sign the amendments.

Authorities routinely rejected the registration applications of NGOs whose names contained the words "human rights," "democracy," "institute," and "society."

On February 19, a Baku court denied registration to the Human Rights Club, which had attempted to register for two years. Experts reported that the ECHR had ruled in four cases over several years that denials of registration by the government violated freedom of association as provided under the European Convention on Human Rights.

The government continued to implement 2011 rules governing a 2009 law that requires foreign NGOs wishing to operate in the country to sign an agreement and reregister with the Ministry of Justice. The foreign NGOs wishing to register their branch in Azerbaijan are required to demonstrate that they support "the Azerbaijani people's national and cultural values" and commit not to be involved in religious and political propaganda. The decree does not specify any time limit for the registration procedure and effectively allows for unlimited discretion of the government to decide whether to register a foreign NGO. With one 2012 exception, no foreign NGOs were able to register with the government according to these rules since 2011.

Some experts estimated that approximately 1,000 NGOs remained unregistered during the year.

c. Freedom of Religion

See the Department of State's *International Religious Freedom Report* at www.state.gov/j/drl/irf/rpt/.

d. Freedom of Movement, Internally Displaced Persons, Protection of Refugees, and Stateless Persons

While the law provides for freedom of movement within the country, foreign travel, emigration, and repatriation, the government at times limited freedom of movement, particularly for internally displaced persons (IDPs).

The government cooperated with the Office of the UN High Commissioner for Refugees (UNHCR) and other humanitarian organizations in providing protection and assistance to IDPs, refugees, returning refugees, asylum seekers, stateless persons, and other persons of concern. The State Migration Service was responsible for all refugee matters, including refugee status determination. International NGOs continued to report that the service remained inefficient and did not operate transparently.

Foreign Travel: Authorities prevented some civil society activists from traveling outside the country. For example, in November authorities prohibited EMDS Chairman Anar Mammadli from traveling to the Eastern Partnership Summit in Vilnius, linking the prohibition to an ongoing investigation into EMDS' alleged tax evasion (see section 3). Authorities also banned the EMDS executive director and the ICV chairman from leaving the country. Since 2006 the government has prevented the foreign travel of Popular Front Party chairman Ali Kerimli by refusing to renew his passport. The government cited an outstanding criminal complaint against him from 1994 as the grounds for the refusal, although it had renewed Kerimli's passport without objection on several occasions since the complaint was filed. All levels of the court system rejected Kerimli's appeal of the decision. In 2009 Kerimli submitted a complaint to the ECHR, which did not hear the case before year's end.

The law requires men of draft age to register with military officials before traveling abroad. Those pursuing higher education may request a deferment to complete their studies. The law on military service does not stipulate deferments for undergraduate or graduate studies although military draft boards commonly granted such deferments upon annual presentation of proof of enrollment. Some travel restrictions were placed on military personnel with access to national security information. Citizens charged with or convicted of criminal offenses and given suspended sentences were not permitted to travel abroad.

While official government policy allows citizens of ethnic Armenian descent to travel, low-level officials reportedly often requested bribes or harassed ethnic Armenians who applied for passports.

Internally Displaced Persons (IDPs)

For the first half of the year, the UNHCR reported 600,336 registered IDPs in the country, representing 153,336 families. The vast majority fled their homes between 1988-93 as a result of the Nagorno-Karabakh conflict.

Initially IDPs were required to register their places of residence with authorities and could live only in approved areas. Historically, this "propiska" registration system, carried over from the Soviet era, was enforced mainly against persons who were forced from their homes after separatists took control of Nagorno-Karabakh and seven other Azerbaijani territories. The government asserted that registration was needed to keep track of IDPs to provide them assistance. According to the Internal Displacement Monitoring Center, many IDPs who resided in Baku were unable to register their residences or gain access to formal employment, government assistance, health care, education, or pensions and had difficulty buying property. Significant numbers of IDPs remained in overcrowded collective centers, where they were socially marginalized with limited employment opportunities and high rates of poverty. Current law no longer requires registration, but it is necessary to obtain IDP status. Temporary registration where IDPs reside does not restrict migration within the country.

The UNHCR reported that, in the first half of the year, the government rehoused

2,704 families, representing approximately 13,520 individuals. The rehousing occurred in the Absheron and Mingachevir regions.

Protection of Refugees

Access to Asylum: The law provides for granting asylum or refugee status, and the government has established a system for providing protection to some refugees through the Refugee Status Determination Department at the State Migration Committee. Although the UNHCR noted some improvements during the year, the country's refugee status determination system did not meet international standards, and the government granted refugee status to only a very small percentage of asylum seekers. The UNHCR recognized 1,500 individuals (asylum seekers, persons of concern to the UNHCR, and refugees recognized under the UNHCR mandate) in the country as of November and provided them with UNHCR letters of protection. According to the State Migration Service, of the 123 persons who applied for refugee status in the first 10 months of the year, eight received refugee status. As in the previous year, the three largest active refugee populations were Chechens, Afghans, and Iranians.

Safe Country of Origin/Transit: According to the UNHCR, Azerbaijan does not allow Russian citizens fleeing the conflict in Chechnya access to the national asylum procedure. The UNHCR noted, however, that the country tolerates the presence of Chechen asylum seekers and accepts the UNHCR's role in providing for their protection and humanitarian needs.

Refoulement: The country subscribes to the principle of nonrefoulement. The government effectively provides territorial protection to persons in need of international protection, despite the lack of a legislative framework providing for complementary protection.

Employment and Access to Basic Services: Most of the approximately 1,000 refugees in the country were not recognized by the government and were under the protection of the UNHCR's mandate. Neither those refugees recognized by the State Migration Committee nor those protected by the UNHCR were allowed to work legally. They also did not have access to social services.

Durable Solutions: The UNHCR noted that the country has not assumed responsibility for the legal protection and subsistence of refugees and asylum seekers.

Temporary Protection: The government has no legal mechanism to provide temporary protection to individuals who do not qualify as refugees. The government accepted the protection letters the UNHCR issued to those it considered refugees. As a result the UNHCR continued to carry out all protection and assistance functions for populations of concern in the country. Despite UNHCR recognition of Chechens, Afghans, and Iranians as populations of concern, the country's laws on residence, registration, and the status of refugees and IDPs do not apply to these persons, who are required to register with police and are not entitled to residence permits.

Stateless Persons

Children derive citizenship by birth within the country or from one's parents. While the law provides for the right to apply for stateless status, some persons could not obtain the documentation required for the application and, therefore, remained formally unrecognized. The law on citizenship makes it difficult for foreigners and stateless persons to obtain citizenship.

According to State Migration Service statistics, there were 1,776 stateless persons in the country in 2012; however, the UNHCR registered only 177. In the first 10 months of the year, 216 stateless persons applied for citizenship, and authorities accepted 163 applications for consideration. The vast majority of stateless persons were ethnic Azeris from Georgia or Iran. NGOs estimated there were many other undocumented stateless persons, with estimates ranging from hundreds to tens of thousands. For the most part, stateless persons enjoy freedom of movement. Nevertheless, because they are without legal status, their access to basic rights, including the right to benefit from public medical services, the right to formal employment, and the right to register marriages, births, and deaths, is limited.

Section 3. Respect for Political Rights: The Right of Citizens to Change Their Government

Although the constitution and law provide citizens with the right to change their government peacefully, the government continued to restrict this right by interfering in the electoral process. The law also provides for an independent legislature; however, the Milli Majlis' independence was constrained and it exercised little legislative initiative independent of the executive branch.

Elections and Political Participation

Recent Elections: The October 9 presidential election fell short of international standards. In their joint October 10 statement of preliminary findings and conclusions, the OSCE's Office for Democratic Institutions and Human Rights (OSCE/ODIHR) and the OSCE Parliamentary Assembly highlighted serious shortcomings that need to be addressed in order for the country to meet its OSCE commitments fully. On election day, OSCE/ODIHR observers witnessed procedural irregularities, including ballot box stuffing, serious problems with vote counting in 58 percent of observed polling stations, and failure to record the number of received ballots. Preceding election day the government also maintained a repressive political environment, which did not provide the fundamental freedoms of assembly, association, and expression necessary for a free and fair electoral competition. Authorities interfered with the media and civil society routinely, sometimes violently interrupted peaceful rallies and meetings before and occasionally during the 22-day campaign period, and jailed a number of opposition and youth activists. Neither the election administration nor the judiciary provided effective redress for appeals. Credible NGOs, such as EMDS, reported similar shortcomings.

EMDS reported on October 23 that the judiciary and all but one Central Election Commission (CEC) member did not engage in due diligence during the postelection grievance process. EMDS also noted that the Constitutional Court accepted the election results four days before the deadline for completing postelection investigations. In its final election report issued December 24, the OSCE/ODIHR highlighted similar flaws. For example, the CEC and the judiciary rejected a postelection complaint submitted by unified opposition candidate Jamil Hasanli due to his submission of photocopies of election observers' affidavits rather than originals as documentation, but the OSCE/ODIHR stated that neither the election code nor CEC instructions required the submission of originals with complaints.

In late October following EMDS' critical postelection statement, authorities opened a criminal investigation of the group and another election monitoring NGO, the ICV, on alleged tax evasion and other charges. On December 16, authorities arrested EMDS Chairman Anar Mammadli and sentenced him to three months' pretrial detention. In response to Mammadli's detention, HRW's senior South Caucasus researcher stated, "By arresting Mammadli, the authorities are sending a message that they are more interested in silencing an inconvenient messenger than investigating credible reports of election fraud." In a December 24 joint statement, 167 public figures in the country called Mammadli a prisoner of conscience and described the charges against him as "trumped up" solely because of his organization's election monitoring.

Authorities took some constructive steps during the election campaign, including the registration of unified opposition candidate Jamil Hasanli, the authorization of some opposition campaign rallies, the decision to invite the OSCE/ODIHR to observe the election, and efficient technical preparation for the election.

Political Parties: While there were 50 registered political parties, the ruling Yeni Azerbaijan Party continued to dominate the political system.   Domestic observers reported that membership in the ruling party conferred advantages, such as preference for public positions.   For the first time since the country's independence, the Milli Mejlis after the 2010 election did not include representatives of the Musavat and Popular Front opposition parties.

Opposition members were more likely to experience official harassment and arbitrary arrest and detention than other citizens.   According to the Human Rights Club, as of October 1, eight political detainees or prisoners were opposition party or movement members.   For example, on March 26, Sumgayit police arrested Popular Front Party youth activist Dashgin Malikov for allegedly possessing a counterfeit banknote.   On July 3, a court sentenced him to two-and-a-half years in prison for illegal possession of drugs.   Local media and NGO sources believed that authorities fabricated the charges against Malikov and in response both to his participation in public protests and to Facebook postings in which he criticized the government. Regional party members often had to conceal the purpose of their gatherings and hold them in remote locations.   Opposition party members reported that police often dispersed small gatherings at tea houses and detained participants for questioning.   Opposition parties continued to have difficulty renting office space, reportedly because landlords were afraid of official retaliation; some parties operated from their leaders' apartments.

Participation of Women and Minorities: There were 19 women in the Milli Mejlis. One woman held a ministerial-level position.   Members of minority groups, such as the Talysh, Avars, Russians, and Jews, served in the Milli Mejlis and in government.

Section 4. Corruption and Lack of Transparency in Government

The law provides criminal penalties for corruption by officials.   While the government made progress prosecuting low- and mid-level corruption, charging 15 individuals with bribery-related offenses in the first 10 months of the year, high-level officials continued to act with impunity.   Transparency International and other observers described corruption as widespread during the year.

Corruption: Beginning in September 2012 and continuing during the year, Elshad Abdullyayev, a parliamentary candidate in 2005 and a former university rector, released several videos implicating government officials in corruption.   One video depicted Abdullayev as a candidate in the 2005 parliamentary elections meeting with then members of parliament Gular Ahmadova and Sevinj Babayeva. Ahmadova was filmed attempting to extort a bribe of $1,000,000 for a parliamentary seat. In the video Ahmadova and Babayeva informed Abdullayev that his previous payment of $500,000 had been delivered to "master Ramiz," which Abdullayev alleged was a reference to the head of the presidential administration, Ramiz Mehdiyev. Following the video's release, authorities opened a criminal investigation against Ahmadova, who was stripped of her seat and later expelled from the ruling New Azerbaijan Party. In December 2012 Babayeva's son announced she died in mysterious circumstances in Turkey. Ahmadova's trial commenced in October, and on December 2, the Baku Court of Grave Crimes sentenced her to three years in prison. During the trial Babayeva's relatives reportedly accused Ahmadova of poisoning her.

Criminal cases related to bribery and other forms of government corruption affecting daily life were initiated during the year, although no senior officials were prosecuted.

There were continued reports that authorities targeted some human rights defenders seeking to combat government corruption. For example, NGOs characterized as politically motivated the February 27 conviction of lawyer Bakhtiyar Mammadov, who had represented families evicted from their homes in Baku, and the continued detention of four anticorruption activists from the Kura NGO arrested in 2012.

Corruption among law enforcement officers was a problem. Despite a decrease in bribe seeking beginning in early 2011, police later returned to their previous practice of levying spurious, informal fines for traffic and other minor violations and extracting protection money from local residents. Low wages continued to contribute to police corruption.

As of October 30, the Ministry of Internal Affairs reported that it investigated 36 cases of corruption and had taken disciplinary action for corruption-related violations against 61 employees, dismissing 36, demoting 21, and issuing official warnings to four.

There was widespread belief that one could pay a bribe for a waiver of military service, which is universal for men between the ages of 18 and 35. Citizens also believed that military personnel could buy assignments to easier military duties for a smaller bribe.

The president and the presidential administration continued a well-publicized program in Baku to decrease corruption at lower levels of public administration. The government established four "ASAN" service centers, which function as one-stop centers for government services, such as birth certificates and marriage licenses, from nine ministries. "ASAN" stands for the Azerbaijan Service and Assessment Network and means "easy" in Azeri.

The Prosecutor General's Office includes an Anticorruption Department (ACD), which nearly tripled in size during the year, authorizing approximately 100 prosecutor and investigator positions. The caseload nearly doubled since 2011, and in the first 10 months of the year, the unit took 153 cases to court and charged 293 people. The ACD also seeks recovery of proceeds from crime. Additionally, the ACD makes recommendations and issues mandatory instructions to eliminate conditions conducive to corruption.

Whistleblower Protection: There is no law specifically providing protection to employees who disclose evidence of illegality.

Financial Disclosure: The law requires officials to submit reports on their financial situation, and the electoral code requires all candidates to submit financial statements. The process of submitting reports is complex and nontransparent, however. Several agencies and bodies are designated recipients, including the Anticorruption Commission, elements of parliament, the Ministry of Justice, and the CEC, but their monitoring role is not well understood. The public does not have access to the reports. The law contemplates only administrative sanctions for noncompliance, but the sanctions are not imposed.

In June 2012 the Milli Mejlis amended the Law on Commercial Secrets to prohibit the public release of the names and capital investment amounts of business founders. Critics claimed the amendments were an attempt to curb investigative journalism into government officials' business interests and could decrease public access to information.

Public Access to Information: Although the law provides for public access to government information by individuals and organizations, the government often did not permit access. Although various government ministries have separate procedures on how to request information, they routinely denied requests, claiming not to possess the information. Individuals have the right to appeal the denials in court, but the courts generally upheld the decisions of the ministries.

Section 5. Governmental Attitude Regarding International and Nongovernmental Investigation of Alleged Violations of Human Rights

A number of domestic and international human rights groups generally operated without government restriction, investigating and publishing their findings on human rights cases. Although the government maintained ties with some human rights NGOs and responded to their inquiries, on occasion it criticized and intimidated other human rights NGOs and activists. The Ministry of Justice continued routinely to deny registration or place burdensome administrative restrictions on human rights NGOs on arbitrary grounds (see section 2.b., Freedom of Association).

During the year a number of NGOs reported increased pressure against their activities. Such pressure took several forms. For example, in contrast to previous years, some NGO representatives reported that they or a family member had been physically assaulted, with impunity. In one high-profile case reported by the Institute for Peace and Democracy's Leyla Yunus, two men reportedly "advised" the 17-year-old son and grandson of human rights NGO leaders to tell him "how to speak in the press," threatened to cut off his tongue to silence his mother, and beat him on July 19. Senior government officials engaged in ad hominem attacks on human rights activists, and in April progovernment media called the recipients of financial assistance from the German Marshall Fund and the National Endowment for Democracy "national traitors."

In March the government spread media articles and television spots accusing the National Democratic Institute's local director of embezzling funds and helping youth movements plot a "Facebook revolution" in connection with the public demonstrations that occurred at that time. The prosecutor general opened a criminal case against the director but later announced that it was closed. The authorities launched a criminal investigation of two election-monitoring NGOs soon after the October presidential election (see section 3).

Some NGOs continued to report that landlords were under pressure not to rent to them. Others reported that hotels would not rent them conference space due to pressure from authorities.

During the year a government council provided 5.3 million manat ($6.6 million) in support to 485 NGOs. While observers considered many of these NGOs progovernment or politically neutral, some NGOs that criticized the government also received grants.

<u>Government Human Rights Bodies</u>:   Citizens may appeal violations committed by the state or by individuals to the ombudsman for human rights, Elmira Suleymanova, or the ombudsman for human rights for the Nakhchivan Autonomous Republic, Ulkar Bayramova.   The ombudsman may refuse to accept cases of abuse that were more than one year old, anonymous, or already being handled by the judiciary.   Human rights NGOs criticized the Ombudsman's Office as lacking independence.

The Ombudsman's Office reported receiving 13,670 complaints during the year, an increase of 9.6 percent from the previous year.   The majority of complaints involved alleged violations of property rights, court provisions for protection of rights and freedoms, social provisions, and housing and labor rights.   Human rights offices in the Milli Mejlis and the Ministry of Justice heard complaints, conducted investigations, and made recommendations to relevant government bodies.

Section 6. Discrimination, Societal Abuses, and Trafficking in Persons

The law prohibits discrimination based on race, gender, disability, language, or social status, but the government did not always respect these prohibitions or effectively enforce them.

Women

<u>Rape and Domestic Violence</u>:   Rape is illegal and carries a maximum sentence of 15 years in prison.   During the year the Ministry of Internal Affairs reported 29 cases of rape, 28 cases of violence of a sexual nature, and 18 cases of sexual violence against a minor.   The rape of a minor, a 13-year-old girl, was reported in Aghdam District.   NGO activists reported that the head of executive power of the district personally obstructed the investigation and protected the alleged perpetrator.

The law establishes a framework for investigation of domestic violence complaints, defines a process to issue restraining orders, and calls for the establishment of a shelter and rehabilitation center for victims.   Some critics of the domestic violence law asserted that a lack of clear implementing guidelines reduced its effectiveness. Despite the law violence against women, including domestic violence, continued to be a problem.   During the year female members of the Milli Mejlis and the head of the State Committee for Family, Women, and Children Affairs increased their activities against domestic violence.   Media coverage of domestic violence issues also began to raise awareness of the problem.

In rural areas women had no effective recourse against assaults by their husbands or others. In Baku a women's crisis center associated with the Institute for Peace and Democracy provided free medical, psychological, and legal assistance to women. The center also worked on a number of projects funded by international donors to combat gender-based violence and trafficking in persons in the Caucasus region. The government ran one shelter providing assistance to victims of trafficking and domestic violence.

Sexual Harassment: While the law prohibits sexual harassment, the government rarely enforced the prohibition. The Ministry of Internal Affairs reported seven cases of sexual harassment during the year. The State Committee for Family, Women, and Children Affairs worked extensively on women's problems, including organizing and hosting several conferences which raised awareness of sexual harassment and domestic violence.

Reproductive Rights: Couples and individuals have the right to decide freely the number, spacing, and timing of their children. Information was accessible so families and individuals could make reproductive decisions free from discrimination, coercion, and violence. Contraception was widely available, but demographic surveys showed low levels of use. Skilled attendance during childbirth was accessible, as was prenatal care and essential obstetric and postpartum care. Patriarchal norms based on cultural, historical, and socioeconomic factors in some cases limited women's reproductive rights.

Discrimination: Although women nominally enjoy the same legal rights as men, societal discrimination was a problem. Traditional social norms and lagging economic development in the country's rural regions continued to restrict women's roles in the economy, and there were reports that women had difficulty exercising their legal rights due to gender discrimination. The law excludes women from certain occupations. The 2013 ILO Committee of Experts on the Application of Standards and Recommendations called on the government to "ensure that any measures limiting women's employment are strictly limited to maternity protection," but the government had not taken action by year's end. Women were underrepresented in high-level jobs, including top business positions.

Gender-based Sex Selection: According to a June study by Marc Michael of New York University's Abu Dhabi campus, the gender ratio of children born in the country was 115 boys for every 100 girls as of the end of 2012. There were reports that gender-based sex selection was widespread, predominantly in rural regions.

Children

Birth Registration: Children derive citizenship by birth within the country or from one's parents.   Registration at birth was routine for births in hospitals or clinics. Some children born at home (for example, to Romani families or those suffering from economic deprivation) were not registered, and statelessness for the children was a problem.   The Ministry of Internal Affairs and the Ministry of Justice continued registering undocumented children after identifying them as a population vulnerable to trafficking.

Education: While education was compulsory, free, and universal until age 17, large families in impoverished rural areas sometimes placed a higher priority on the education of male children and kept girls in the home to work.   Some poor families forced their children to work or beg rather than attend school.   A Baku NGO working with street children reported that boys and girls engaged in street begging and prostitution.

Child Abuse: During the year the Ministry of Internal Affairs reported six cases of rape involving underage victims, 18 cases of sexual violence against minors, and three cases of immoral acts against minors.

Forced and Early Marriage: Under the age of consent law, a girl can legally marry at age 18 and, with the local authorities' permission, at age 17.   The law further states that a boy can marry at age 18.   In 2002 the Caucasus Muslim Board defined 18 as the marriage age, but the fatwa failed to have much effect on religious marriage contracts (kabin or kabin-nama).

The criminal code establishes fines of 3,000 to 4,000 manat ($3,750 to $5,000) or imprisonment of up to four years for the crime of forced marriage with underage children.

NGOs reported that the number of early marriages continued to increase.   Girls who married under the terms of religious marriage contracts were of particular concern, since these evade governmental oversight and do not entitle the wife to recognition of her status in case of divorce.   The Social Union of Solidarity among Women reported numerous instances in which men moved to Russia for work, leaving their underage wives in Azerbaijan.

Sexual Exploitation of Children: The law prohibits pornography, and its production, distribution, or advertisement is punishable by three years' imprisonment.   Statutory rape is defined as "the sexual relations or other actions of a sexual nature, committed by a person who has reached 18, with a person who has not reached 16" and is punishable by up to three years' imprisonment.   The recruitment of minors for the purpose of prostitution (involving a minor in immoral acts) is punishable by a sentence of three to five years, although the presence of such aggravating factors as violence could increase the potential sentence to five to eight years.   In 2013 the Ministry of Internal Affairs reported one case involving the trafficking of a minor for sexual exploitation and two cases involving the recruitment of minors for prostitution.

Displaced Children: A large number of refugee and IDP children lived in substandard conditions.   In some cases these children were unable to attend school. During the year the government reported that it spent 628 million manat ($785 million) on assistance to IDPs, primarily for housing, health care, and education. The government stated that it spent approximately 4.5 billion manat ($5.6 billion) on assistance to IDPs since early 2008.

International Child Abductions: The country is not a party to the 1980 Hague Convention on the Civil Aspects of International Child Abduction.

Anti-Semitism

There were no credible reports of anti-Semitic acts against the country's Jewish community, which numbered between 20,000 and 30,000 individuals.

Trafficking in Persons

See the Department of State's *Trafficking in Persons Report* at www.state.gov/j/tip/.

Persons with Disabilities

The law prohibits discrimination against persons with physical, sensory, intellectual, and mental disabilities in employment, education, air travel and other transportation, access to health care, or the provision of other state services, but the government did not enforce these provisions effectively.   Employment discrimination remained a problem.   Employers generally hesitated to hire persons with disabilities.   A common belief persisted that children with disabilities were ill and needed to be separated from other children and institutionalized, but special education facilities were available to children with certain disabilities.   Several international and local NGOs facilitated educational campaigns to change social perceptions and reintegrate children with disabilities.   There were no laws mandating access to public or other buildings, information, or communications for persons with disabilities, and most buildings were not accessible.

Conditions in facilities for persons with mental and other disabilities varied; some provided adequate care, while in others qualified staff, equipment, and supplies were inadequate to maintain sanitary conditions and provide a proper diet.

The Ministry of Health and the Ministry of Labor and Social Welfare are responsible for protecting the rights of persons with disabilities.

National/Racial/Ethnic Minorities

Some of the approximately 20,000 to 30,000 citizens of Armenian descent living in the country faced discrimination in employment, housing, and the provision of social services. Citizens who were ethnic Armenians often concealed their ethnicity by legally changing the ethnic designation in their passports. There were no reports of violence against Armenians during the year.

Some groups reported sporadic incidents of discrimination, restrictions on their ability to teach in their native languages, and harassment by local authorities. These groups included Talysh in the south, Lezghi in the north, and Meskhetians and Kurds.

Societal Abuses, Discrimination, and Acts of Violence Based on Sexual Orientation and Gender Identity

Antidiscrimination laws exist but do not specifically enumerate lesbian, gay, bisexual, and transgender (LGBT) individuals. Societal intolerance, violence, and discrimination based on sexual orientation and gender identity remained a problem.

A local NGO reported that there were numerous incidents of police brutality against individuals based on sexual orientation but noted that authorities did not investigate or punish those responsible. A local NGO reported at least eight police raids directed at LGBT persons in the first 10 months of the year. From March through September, police arrested at least 41 LGBT persons on charges of illegal possession of drugs, with possible sentences of three to four years' imprisonment. Additionally, specific police stations were known to extort money from gay individuals in return for not disclosing their orientation.

LGBT individuals continued to refuse to lodge formal complaints with law enforcement bodies due to fear of social stigma, reprisal, or retaliatory repression.

According to the NGO International Gay and Lesbian Human Rights Commission, the country's gay population had been "intimidated to the point of invisibility."

One NGO worked on LGBT issues, including the prevention of HIV/AIDS and the provision of legal advice, psychological assistance, and outreach activities. The NGO reported no official harassment of its work. Baku activists held a small gay pride event on September 13; there were no reports of violence or harassment in connection with the event.

There was societal prejudice against LGBT persons. While dismissing an employee for reasons related to sexual orientation is illegal, LGBT individuals reported that employers found other reasons to dismiss them. Discrimination in access to health care was also reportedly a problem. Additionally, some groups used allegations of LGBT orientation to smear opponents. For example, progovernment demonstrators verbally attacked an opposition leader, incorrectly portraying him as gay. On September 28, presidential candidate Hafiz Hajiyev repeated these allegations during a televised pre-election debate and verbally attacked LGBT persons.

Other Societal Violence or Discrimination

There were no reports of societal violence or discriminations against persons with HIV/AIDS.

Section 7. Worker Rights

a. Freedom of Association and the Right to Collective Bargaining

The law, including related regulations and statutes, provides for freedom of association, including the right to form independent labor unions. Uniformed military and police are prohibited from joining unions. The law also prohibits managerial staff from joining unions, but managers in government industries often had union dues automatically deducted from their paychecks. The law allows unions to conduct their activities without government interference. There were no reported cases of government interference, but union leaders generally cooperated closely with the government, and international observers judged that unions represented the interests of their members poorly. The law provides most workers with the right to strike. Categories of workers prohibited from striking include high-ranking executive and legislative officials; law enforcement officers; court employees; fire fighters; and health, electric power, water supply, telephone, railroad, and air traffic control workers. Striking workers who disrupt public transportation could be sentenced to up to three years in prison. The law prohibits retribution against strikers, such as dismissal or replacement. The law also prohibits discrimination against trade unions and labor activists. The law provides workers with the right to bargain collectively; however, unions could not effectively negotiate wage levels and working conditions because government-appointed boards ran major state-owned firms and set wages for all government employees. The law requires the reinstatement of workers fired for union activity. A local NGO reported that many large companies routinely reinstated workers on short-term contracts. The law does not prohibit trade unions from carrying out political activities. Restrictions on trade unions' associating with or receiving finances from political parties exist, although this provision was not uniformly enforced.

Although the labor law applies to all workers and enterprises, the government can negotiate bilateral agreements that effectively exempt multinational enterprises from national labor laws. For example, production-sharing agreements (PSAs) between the government and multinational energy enterprises did not provide for employee participation in a trade union. Labor organizations and local NGOs reported that some of these companies discouraged employees from forming unions, and most employees of multinational enterprises operating under PSAs were not union members, although there were exceptions. Workers employed by British Petroleum were unionized, but the situation was worse in other multinational corporations, especially companies with third-country subcontractors.

The Azerbaijan Trade Unions Confederation (ATUC) was the only trade union confederation in the country. The trade union registration process is cumbersome, and although ATUC was registered as an independent organization, some workers considered it closely aligned with the government.

There were some restrictions, such as increased bureaucratic scrutiny, on the right to form unions and conduct union activities. Most unions were not independent. The overwhelming majority of them remained tightly linked to the government, with the exception of some journalists' unions. Both local and international NGOs claimed that workers in most industries were largely unaware of their rights and afraid of retribution if they initiated complaints. This was especially true for workers in the public sector.

Collective bargaining agreements were often treated as formalities and not enforced. ATUC, which only has access to its affiliates, reported that at the start of 2012 it represented 1.6 million members in 26 sectors. If a company is not a member of ATUC, responsibility falls to the Ministry of Labor and Social Protection. ATUC stated that in 2012 it received approximately 149,174 appeals and resolved 98.6

percent of them. It reportedly helped 670 persons appeal their dismissal from work, of which 172 individuals were reinstated. Each year ATUC signs a tripartite agreement with the Council of Ministers and the Confederation of Enterprises. Many of the state-owned enterprises that dominated the formal economy withheld union dues from workers' pay but did not deliver the dues to the unions. Employers officially withheld a quarter of the dues collected for the oil workers' union for "administrative costs" associated with running the union. Moreover, a complete lack of transparency made it impossible to tell exactly how dues were spent. Unions and their members had no recourse to investigate withheld funds. Legislation prohibits employers from impeding the collective bargaining process; however, employers engaged in activities restricting collective bargaining such as subcontracting and use of short-term employment agreements.

Membership in the Union of Oil and Gas Industry Workers remained mandatory for the State Oil Company's 65,200 workers, and authorities automatically deducted union dues (2 percent of each worker's salary) from their paychecks.

b. Prohibition of Forced or Compulsory Labor

The law prohibits all forms of forced or compulsory labor, except in circumstances of war or in the execution of a court's decision under the supervision of a government agency. Migrant workers were subjected to conditions of forced labor in the construction industry. Forced begging of children was a problem and domestic servitude of Filipina trafficking victims was an emerging problem. Men and boys were subjected to conditions of forced labor within the country. While they stated that some progress was made, local NGOs believed that overall the government did not enforce the law effectively. During the year the antitrafficking department within the Ministry of Internal Affairs inspected construction and agricultural sector sites, but did not identify any victims of labor trafficking. In February, however, a court for the first time convicted a labor trafficking offender with a sentence of eight and a half years' imprisonment.

Also see the Department of State's *Trafficking in Persons Report* at www.state.gov/j/tip/.

c. Prohibition of Child Labor and Minimum Age for Employment

The minimum age for employment depended on the type of work. In most instances the law permits children to work from age 15; children who are 14 may work in family businesses or, with parental consent, in daytime after-school jobs that pose no hazard to their health. Children under 16 may not work more than 24 hours per week; children between the ages of 16 and 17 may not work more than 36 hours per week. The law prohibits employing children under 18 in difficult and hazardous work conditions and identifies specific work and industries from which children are barred, including work with toxic substances and underground, at night, in mines, and in nightclubs, bars, casinos, or other businesses that serve alcohol. The Ministry of Labor and Social Security is responsible for enforcing child labor laws. Although the ministry conducted inspections during the year, a local NGO reported the need for increased monitoring.

There were few complaints of abuses of child labor laws during the year, although there were anecdotal reports of child labor in agriculture and street work.

d. Acceptable Conditions of Work

The national minimum wage was 105 manat ($131) per month. The average poverty line during the year was 116 manat ($145) per month, with 125 manat ($156) the level for able-bodied persons, 94 manat ($118) for pensioners, and 93 manat ($116) for children. The law requires equal pay for equal work regardless of gender, age, or other classification.

The law provides for a 40-hour workweek; the maximum daily work shift is 12 hours. Workers in hazardous occupations may not work more than 36 hours per week. The law requires lunch and rest periods, which are determined by labor contracts and collective agreements. It was not known whether local companies provided the legally required premium compensation for overtime, although international companies generally did. There is no prohibition on excessive compulsory overtime. Most individuals worked part time in the informal economy, where the government did not enforce contracts or labor laws.

The law provides equal rights to foreign and domestic workers. Local human rights groups, including the Oil Workers Rights Defense Council, an NGO dedicated to protecting worker rights in the oil sector, maintained that employers, particularly foreign oil companies, did not always treat foreign and domestic workers equally. Domestic employees of foreign oil companies often received lower pay and worked without contracts or health care.

While the law sets health and safety standards, government inspection of working conditions by the Ministry of Labor and Social Protection's labor inspectorate was weak and ineffective, and employers widely ignored standards. The ATUC monitored compliance with labor and trade regulations, including safety and health conditions. Violations of acceptable conditions of work in the construction and oil and gas sectors remained problematic. The ATUC reported good cooperation with Russian and Georgian authorities on measures to protect Russian and Georgian migrant workers' rights and the safety of working conditions. The Ministries of Labor and Internal Affairs reportedly monitored the labor rights of other workers in hazardous sectors and in the informal economy (unregistered businesses), which accounts for between 10 and 30 percent of the economy.

There were occasional protests of labor conditions. On March 25, for example, employees of the Gabala-based Azeri Trans company held a protest demanding that the company pay their salaries, provide better working conditions, and sign labor contracts. On April 1, police detained labor activists Tehran Musayev, Aydin Aliverdiyev, and Siyavush Yaraliyev for participating in the protest. The court detained Musayev and Yaraliyev for six days and Aliverdiyev for four days before releasing them.

According to the Oil Workers Rights Defense Council, there were 15 deaths and 42 complaints of on-the-job injuries, including the failure to pay allowances, during the year.

ATUC reported 52 industrial injuries and 24 deaths in 2012, with 10 of the deaths in the oil and energy sectors. A local NGO estimated there were 82 industrial deaths, of which 36 were in construction. ATUC and Ministry of Labor officials inspected worksites, particularly in the construction, energy, and oil sectors, and recommended improvements in labor conditions to employers.